RECIPE NOTEBOOK

illustrated
by

JOANNA ISLES

Recipes by

Aleah Osaba

First published in 1991 by Pavilion Productions Ltd
A division of Pavilion Books Ltd
196 Shaftesbury Avenue, London WC2H 8JL
Copyright © Joanna Isles 1991
Designed by Joanna Isles
Printed and bound in Italy by L.E.G.O.

ISBN 1 85145 690 2

CONTENTS

HOW TO USE THIS BOOK

This recipe notebook has been specially designed to be a record of favourite recipes. For easy reference it is divided into categories which can be found on the contents page. At the back, there is space for personal notes, extra recipes or cooking tips.

Once the book is filled up with recipes, some of the pages at the back can also be used to make an index.

meat
POULTRY
game

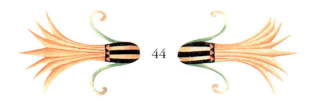

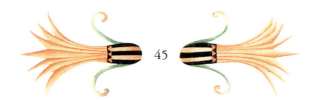

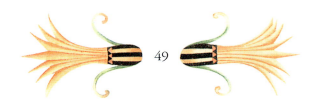

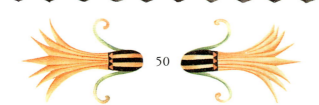

vegetables

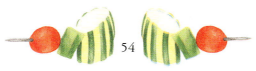

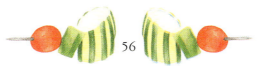

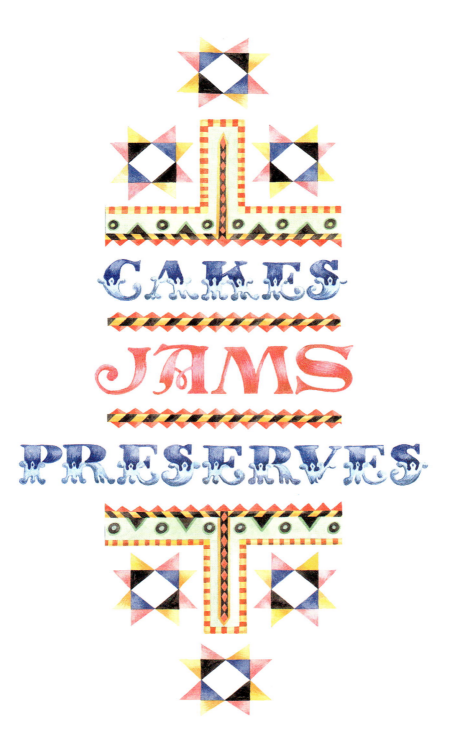

68

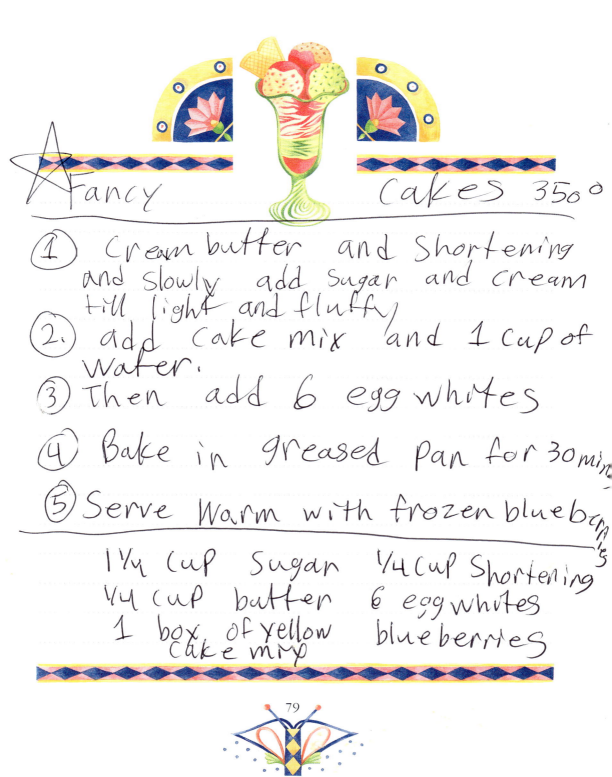

Fancy Cakes 350°

1. Cream butter and shortening and slowly add sugar and cream till light and fluffy

2. add cake mix and 1 cup of water.

3. Then add 6 egg whites

4. Bake in greased pan for 30 min.

5. Serve warm with frozen blueberries

1¼ cup sugar   ¼ cup shortening
¼ cup butter   6 egg whites
1 box of yellow   blueberries
   cake mix

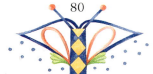

80

Notes

Notes

Notes

Notes

Notes

Notes

Notes

Notes